T0078078

DJT:
Directionless Jumping Train

Bill F. Ndi

Langaa Research & Publishing CIG
Mankon, Bamenda

Publisher
Langaa RPCIG
Langaa Research & Publishing Common Initiative Group
P.O. Box 902 Mankon
Bamenda
North West Region
Cameroon
Langaagrp@gmail.com
www.langaa-rpcig.net

Distributed in and outside N. America by African Books Collective
orders@africanbookscollective.com
www.africanbookscollective.com

ISBN-10: 9956-551-08-2

ISBN-13: 978-9956-551-08-8

Dedication

To the eighty plus million Americans who have chosen to be on the right side of History especially when the train of unity in diversity had been hijacked by a mad train driver with a sleazy sloganeering appeal to dimwits and is such that, "… ignite the engine of hatred/ He refuses to recognize."

Preface

A nightmare, lasting a minute, might take one through a lifetime of hell. *DJT: Directionless Jumping Train* takes one through a nightmarish train ride of biblical and epic proportion; echoing the doomsday promise of an eternal hellfire in which to burn. Set in Vespucci's find, this nightmarish train ride has dragged on for four years. DJT is driven by a lunatic for whom God had made a mistake to have created a multi-colored tableau with one of his brush stroke leaving a black stain on his cherished snow-white canvas. Consequently, God must be politicized, legalized, and every shred of decency must be thrown overboard; leaving stones crying out of the walls of The White House.

DJT, the nightmare is just one sentence spun over 1450 lines as the author's venture into numerology; an attempt that would flabbergast those who believe in the irrational science of numbers. The sentence traverses and portrays the US through multiple political optics surrounded by social chaos gliding on the rails of hatred, provoking anger and using name-calling as a shield to base covetousness. Read the sentence not as a grammatical sentence but the time served for one's crimes and the number forty-five as the mark of the beast whose efforts and endeavors amount to zero. Also, the zero flags the deceitful baseness and nothingness of his attempt to highjack the providential goodness of the gift to the melting pot that the pilgrims, even with their foibles, legated to posterity while highlighting the poet's own refusal to grant the criminal and mad train driver respite by punctuating the sentence.

The fiendishly winding sentence expresses a natural aversion to the erratic stance of a mad hate monger. *DJT* takes a one-way voyage-like course and transforms the tone into a virulent refutation of hate mongering and fear stoking through the urgency with which the speaker hastes the end of the crazy train ride. The flashbacks and speed acceleration in the months leading up to and maybe after the US 2020 elections account for the wide range of references that underscore *DJT*'s poignancy.

DJT: Directionless Jumping Train

Cynical to service
Uncouth to heroism
And a knave to green backs
As both heroism
And service with no fiscal
Tilt is but a delight
To suckers and losers
Leaving penman
After penman
Pen-woman
After
Pen-woman
Pen-girl
After
Pen-girl
Pen-boy
After
Pen-boy
Penning and penning all
About his jumping train
With no bearing at break neck
Speed headed
For a gigantic wreck
Out of which we wish none go
To seek a shattered black body
'Coz in this world he vied to save the day
He was spited and ridiculed
The best thought of him nothing but fun
Out of which to carve out
A one-term leaseholder
Who denied to be one and was replaced

By a lousy mad machinist
Sent straight from the hellish hearth
And abetted by Reagan's evil empire
For in him rest a craven coward
Whose claim to wisdom
And genius tells lies untold
From whence our world was spoken
Into existence and long before
Sparking the ire of that choicest confidant
Who to defy master maker
Would he his mutiny staged
To win his rulership over
The fallen of which one fell
In the United States of America
Of which he would the divided states
Craft and his chest thump
For having nothing for which
To apologize
Neither to God nor to man
He kneads as dough to get nuts
And let stink every breath
Of lies
Scaring to death compliant flies
As he attracts the unruly
Willing to follow mortal remains
Beneath the stele
Into their last abode
And all for a fake crown carrier
From the nether world sent
To wreck the train pilgrims
Set on rails in their quest to be free
And who having freedom found
Embraced the angels of yore

Falling in for fame
And ushering celebrity con artist
To becoming their crime boss
For whom a bullet they would take
And sandpaper every one
Of his bumpy edges
Sign posting the monster
At the wheel thirsting for blood
And playing the bad boy card
Of his followers' enemies
He has trumped and whipped up
Their boiling pot of anger
On which he has a lid fastened
As they have accepted to jump
Into the moving locomotive's boiler
In their hunger for coal
In a world where it is but an antique
Predating Caesar's Rome
And Pharaohs' Egypt
In which the heat of cruelty
Ventured in Kubla Khan's
Measureless caverns to man
Wherein forty-five is embolden
To grab the opposite sex
Like Gilgamesh ravishing a bride
On her wedding day before the groom
And making a mockery of his creator
Breeding lies in the train
He drives with lies after lies
To stir the waters muddy
In an expert bid to shift blames
Onto Muddy Waters for wailing
Out his Blues

At the sign of which slam-dunking
The rock bottom
The wrecker in chief steps
On the accelerator to confirm
The pit bottomless
And his train one to downplay
A pandemic with goals
To populate the burning furnace
He vies strives and hopes he inherits
From the master of devious art
Quick to offer the world
He is trying to steal
To the son of the real owner
With a daring condition
He submits to his ill will
Which inspires to kill
Steal and destroy the oneness
Of a tableau enriched
With multiple colors
And painted by The Hand
That feeds without demur
And not such that mocks
To steal the show for earthly glory
Thackeray Make Peace
Would we left behind
For the sake of some sense
And sensibility with which to bail
America out of pride and prejudice
Her full trainload
Unloaded on innocence
Blake composed his songs about
Before settling to muse on experience
Which as most would claim is the best

Teacher turns our melting pot
On her head never to learn
From history to substantiate
The gospels' claim of nothing
New under the sun moon and stars
Shining light in the dark
Crevices of man's hidden agenda
On which he would he were his own
Maker and his Maker's maker
Bathing in opulence of arrogance
Spite and condescension for the will
And door none born of a woman
Can break nor open and close
And not even with claims
i and i alone can fix it
When the i spent his life
In the business of conning the poor
The rich and the state
And with hands that kill
Everything they touch
And yet Pilgrims' offspring refuse to revisit
Ancient Greece with zeal to enrage
Apollo to inflict a donkey's ears
To forebears' labors
After three hundred and ninety-seven
Earthly revolution on its axis
During which time offspring dreamt
Of a magical potion to make
Trinkets bling bling shoving aside
William's merchant of Venice
Whose choice of casket won him a bride
Not because such glittered as gold
But for its weight worth the world

In more than gold
The sparkle of which sent brutes West
And had their brutishness
Help John Wayne engrave his name
On popular memory in that wild
Wild West that's the horse on which
To ride and leave a dust track on a road
Walked by a man pushed to invisibility
But willing to cling on to his guitar
And sound the whistle of this train
Passing by the Barracoon
In which the last black cargo
Was drop and left with nothing
But eyes to watch God
And trade twelves
In hope to fly home
One day and land far away
From Ellison's infernal Harlem
Of Shadow and Act
That would have us going to the territory
To have a black laugh
And not sing praises in a train
With a choirmaster whose hooded
Tongue allows him to speak
With both sides of his mouth
Spitting out venom to blind Conrad
Who would readily find in his own world
The heart of darkness
To the core for there all lives
Matter except that which is black
As if to suggest looting and chaos
The engine in the Western train
Running off its rails to accuse

Peaceful protesters they abuse
Brand
Maim
Slay
Kill
Blame
And name
Them
Violent anarchist
For in their dream time
Justice echoes and echoes
From a digeridoo
To have them in the name of this sound
Dare stand up against injustice
With wish to have peace reign
Upon the face of the universe
Hijacked and buried in the entrails
Of bottomless pit bound freight
Hasting the departure from the bench
Of the no nonsense heroine
Of Ibsen's *A Doll's House*
Willing to put to shame
A handpicked bunch
Under Durham scheme
To turn around and heap blames
Through a charade the speed of light
Must drive out into the playing
Of the proverbial October surprise
By a faithful who has made of fear
A weapon of choice
To target suburban women
His hands can only reach for their pussies
As he has done time without number

And this time must have them use theirs
To enthrone him and make him strongman
He has always admired and wanted to be
To the point where he is willing to trade his nation
Not Ellison's twelves of which he has no knowledge
And had he such his understanding would ally
With his deplorables who seem to fancy
Their end a glorious one far from Danté
And closer to a certain Vanessa
Who'd taken Paradise for last name
Not anywhere near the two Americas
Wherein the haves frown at the tripod
On which stand the motto
Liberty
Equality
Fraternity
As they burn with desire
To embrace a fraternal order of brutes
Who brace themselves with license
To murder and no knowledge
Of the balancing act of keeping safe
And giving train riders a smooth
And blissful ride to a destination
Where heads can with sycophantic
Nods self-greet and play the agama
Lizards themselves
Giant gators dragging lions with them
Into the swamp and making them
New dwellers for photo opportunities
During which the abysmal king delights
To pose with all who'd not
Have any Black Hand defile
Their blood painted greenbacks

Or the green lawns in their back yards
Whereon the king misquotes the scriptures
Holding them upside-down
Believing to oppress is to rule
To divide to unite
White
Nationalists against the plea
To bring all into the fold
Wherein the ilk of Georgia's number
Seventy-five who disbanded business
And flung the store keys
With outrage far beyond the deep sea
For he wondered how jaguars
Could shepherd white sheep
By the foothills of the Rocky
And thinly veiled capitol
Now accused of porous leaks
With no hedges to stop
An inevitable crash down the valley
Which their cast would a rift
Defies Ngugi's with a river between
Without any to make life viable
And displease the con-tested rogue
Garbed in crime from head to toe
To show too much and never enough
Of the way one family created
In the stead of love
That monster
Saying and doing anything
About everything
To leave this nation sand-blind
With his love for crimespiracy
Decried in Rage

Fear

Fire and Fury

In the room where it happened

At the sight

Of the devil's bargain

And the generation of vipers

Teaming and not forgetting warning

Words from his mouth

Are all lies

And tell everything he touches dies

At the hands of his greed

Ambition

And corruption

At work to make things worse

In ways none would think

To make truth tellers

Liars

As well as witnesses

Leakers

And all opponents against the monster's ideas

Liberals

Vying and dying

To taste of the blood

Of the cold blooded swamp

Dwelling kleptopian

Genius

In this train where it all happened

And is happening

Under fire not to unmake

America as once was the red union

Card castle pulling her weight

With a politburo

Which came down under the flicker

Of a child's finger
And birthed a cold calculating machine
Whose engine throb
Has hungered and hungers
To derail
Our train in vain
Till now that he's found a willing
And desirous Power monger
To be made beholden to him
With a consent decree
Never to bad talk Yeltsin's savior
Who now coaches his knave
On power tricksterism
And one of which ways is to push
Facts till they embrace
Salvador Dali
And craft the political stage
Into a new crime form
Stealing from art to marvel
Marveling by pushing the bounds
Of the reel beyond the real
To rattle senses and appeal
To the worst beastly instincts
Chiseled out of fear for the unarmed
To whom this train wreck
Would the world turn upside
Down and leave them
In a dire trumpocratic straits
Bleaker than Dickens'
House
And harder than Times
At the Stone Lodge
Bashing all hopes

Grading and grinding expectations
For greater and better days
Ahead to stamp out the stamped
Who from the beginning counted
Not as one and when counted
Never was enfranchised with a vote
They know would weed out
The dangerously irresponsible
Deplorable
Taking aim at scientific
Truths with tall tales
Of lengthy shadows
Haunting
    And
Hunting
Him with long
Double barrel canons
Pointing at him charlatan
Unable to take the heat
From his lying conscience
Whose tempestuous torture
Pushes emotional currents
On a roller coaster
Train ride
Echoing the prevailing virus
With which every wake up
Brings to bear something new
In to the wrong train
Whose wheel is entrusted
To the Insane
And his acolytes
Poisoning the air with inanities
A cobra would spit out

To blind its prey
And help the helper thrown
Under the train
With claims facts are misspeaks
When his every breath wreaks of lies
That would not attract flies
Save the stubborn and willing
To follow
Corpses in to the grave
Before coming to terms
With the surreal reality
Of boarding a mad train
And heeding a mad train pilot
Who jibbers and lay claims
To speaking Greek and Latin
Only Aristotle and Aristophanes
Would come close to deciphering
King Arthur as he lay dying
And only the dying man could tell
The old order changeth
Yielding place to the new
Rejoicing in deterioration
The batch of honor
The new era wears
To brag about
And impose his insane curriculum
With the sole aim of distorting
History while embracing
Nationalism
In guise of patriotism
Which to Sartre is but a commitment
To bring out all
Hidden skeletons

From the cupboard
To name
And shame
The culprits disposed
To convolute and pollute
With a blizzard of tongue twisting
Arm twisting
Back breaking
Head and heart aching
Ruse and lies blown in from the steppes
Where golden hair Belphegor
Hopes to nip Genghis Khan
Before he comes to battle
His way out of the romantic chasm
And instead of building
The pleasure dome
He'd build the guillotine wall
Besides which he'd erect
Cages for children
Hacked out of the mothers' wombs
Because these good Christians
Are pro-lifers
And cannot fathom
Their creator's mistake
In coloring the face of His universe
With dyes He in His omniscience
Failed to capture for the irritant
They must highlight
And give *daibolos* his quarter-moon-smile
In his rush to leave history
In a postmodern
Anachronistic twist
Pretending citizens need not

The mask they must wear
When Milton pulls human ears
To show them how their light is spent
With no consideration for the question
Of whiteness while holding
On to Dickinson's
Standing-
Loaded canons
If we must die blind
To seeing the world
In a grain of sand
And heaven in a flower
That bloomed in the heart
Of the stylist and manicurist
Of the garden of justice
Wherein she laid a bedrock
Of principle to hedge in
The jumping train
Sweeping all on his journey
Down the valley
Of the shadow of death
With no memory
In her long solitary
Journey she found refuge
In the shadow of the most high
In whom she now
Rest in perfect peace
While the mad driver in glee
Drools like a child
In a candy store
Looking for tooth decay
That would get off the rails
The mad elephant train

Shifting gears from political
Representation
To that of non-representation
Against which blood had watered
And whetted the appetite
For the longing
Of the motion and power
Vested in the people
Who fought and flooded
Tons of tea
To stop the monarchical
Train in which the fierce throated
And scaly Mar-a-Lago gator
In escape from the seat of Lady
Liberty
Having seen the latter in tears
And with hers having bred fears
Conjures the new wool
With which to spin
Threads for the fabric of the base
Life drunk with greed
And hypocritical hate
Directed at truth revealers
For having the spine
And being fearless
To ask questions
And have their names
Dragged and drowned in a cesspool
They wish to dredge
In hope their names
In the mud dragged
Stir Whitman in his tomb
And carve a frown

From his smile
At a winter locomotive
The nature of which he'd
Not measured
Seeing serpentine fumes
Bemuse the swamp dweller
And goad him
To haul the foolishness
Perpetually permeating
The Deep South
With applauses his strides
Are the greatest in taking passengers
Five centuries behind
Throwing overboard
Everything gain and nourishment
Those centuries brought on the table
Around which all could see
Pellucid recklessness
Dancing to hurricane's
Mad music
Snouted and coughed out
Of a trans-Siberian locomotive
Borrowed from Transylvania
For a Stone Mountain Horror Show with the count
Of divided kay cube states
Knocking at the door of each
And every tomb in the churchyard
Where he has faith fools
On the leashes of pro-life
For children in the womb
And womb alone
Not after they are born
To this world of sin

Wherein they must their bane
Shoulder to give wings
To that lord of the flies
To fly sky high
While they bring down
Workers and soldiers
To pay for their foolishness
In service
Wherein they sowed seeds
Of the fruits they must reap
To follow the prescription
Of divine order
In which the discord they fomented
Now comes to haunt
Them with them being so blessed
With the worst of their kind
Who never courage had to stand
The draft but must now his chest
Puff out and float nowhere near
The offspring of the great
Catherine who enlightenment
Embraced and welcomed Voltaire
To show her the window
To the West leading the way
To peaceful revolution
Her heir has now ditched
For the shortcut to violence
Making BLM peaceful protests
An impossibility
With vigilante justice
And vigilante killers
Hailed heroes at seventeen
And one good enough to shepherd

Sunset mongers into the new era
Of infective chimera
Out to slay and bury
Diversity
With trumpublicans embracing
Disraeli's two nations
And two speed law
Crafted to appease
The palate of an empty
Question dodging
Vessel
Embarked on his hurricane
Aftermath fantasy
In which delusions
He'd celebrate
Just when the world
Looks on espousing thoughts
Of having men
With ripe balls
And hardened kernels in their sac
With which to resist
Their choicest volcanic
Liar who spews hot lava lies
Directly from Erta Ale
Who was and is
The cradle of the Big bang
That burned the first man
Black and let him shine
In Truth and glow in Honesty
Proven to be bitter pills
For the wicked rapacious vulture
courting
lies

kissing
lies
breathing
lies
farting
lies
pooping
lies
burping
lies
coughing
lies
sweating
lies
telling
lies
drinking
lies
peeing
lies
blinking
lies
and does nothing without
lies
all on which he feasts
ignoring a zillion cries
from the now resurrected
John Waywards
and chimney sweeping coffin dwellers
sweeping the ogres' to wealth
and theirs to no health
making of them nothing else
but penury minting machines

whose errands are thankless
and would only invoke Sir Walter's
Soul on his to give everyone
And our uneducated potentate with ambition
Not a lie
but the Sartrian ugly face
Of the mess with which
he's painted his drifting locomotive
and vouches for continuation
not transition
as he knows in any game
fair and square
he loses and as such
and fearing he'd himself find
where he chanted he'd have a woman
contender in jumpsuit
he'd rather pull the train
off its rails
and send people home early
if they cower not to him
taking his cruel madness
for sanity and strength
making him strongman
he'd always wanted to be
long before a coach
he found in the red square
and one who in turn has had one dream
and only one dream
to avenge his soviet death
and bring down the bald eagle
and be reckoned
the only cock in the barn
to crow and alert it was time

for the tides to turn the tables
and give a foretaste served cold
after a war of this name
to the empire that dubbed his mother
the evil empire and the time
is now with the eaglets flying
with hawks and taking this borrowed
train headed to Count Dracula's Castle
as they are enticed by the root
of all evil they see as a saving grace
that has dragged businessmen
in cassocks laying claims to being
those of God serving lesser gods
to tempting the Lord our God
and worshipping earthly
trinkets Chaucer had damned
questing what iron will do
if gold rust as do these rotten
apples who 'bide not by the good
they show as they do the booty
they loot as if by bread alone man lives
which is so the reverse of man's
instruction from the master
whose emblems
humility and honesty
are now thrown and crushed
underneath the rails
alongside the only voice
people have to choose how to die
compounding murder with a lie
to color the streets with anger
which suits the narrative of bigotry
against the Five Starred Red Flag

used to whitewash the carpet
adorning the road to and from
the crime boss's Red Square dacha
wherefrom he pulls the strings
to send a madman Whitman
would never call Captain
and not even with a lower case
for he is a sad case
thinking to hear America singing
is to mute and scare brothers and sisters
whom he claims are of color
and which claim drives home
thoughts of the train boarders
and passengers in a brakeless ride
turned Dambissa Forest
Chibok girls
In their odyssey
A long way from home
During which the wind comes
Singing of a prentice
Divine rights knight
Looting and burning
The last hope in Democracy
Vaping
Destroying
Stilling
And
Stealing
From the young
Before they grow to call
Vaper
Destroyer
Stiller

And thief
To order with chants
Of vote him out
And honor her last wish
during which he pretends
to pay his last respect
to our fallen icon
of our broken scale
and one that had shouldered
the weight of injustice
and had leveled it with justice
which the train driving disciple
of Leo XIII
and his dogma of kingly infallibility
would call a far cry
and too rowdy to be heard
by his imperial creed
as he addresses men
of the fourth estate
he'd often decried in Ibsenian
terms painting them boogeymen
against which the people
should all rise for they could
hear what the people's lover
hard of hearing and deaf
not to speak of his selectiveness
in hearing refuses to hear
with his every deceptive
temptation
and attractive
promise
with a shiny gold look alike
chocolate bar

with which he baits
Roosevelt's children of the crucible
Whose world is rife
With antagonism
Enflamed by the divider in chief
Whose only desire is to joy-ride
The train into the ditch
With a malicious smirk
Believing it the way
To salvage his Hitlerian stranglehold
From the melting pot
In which diversity has simmered
To crystalize our democracy
Into the finest jewel caught by an eye
That sees way beyond
The ephemeral I
That ushers-in isolation
Carting ism as doctrine
Flying only to replicate
Vladimir Ilyich Ulyanov
(aka Lenin's) brainchild's
Fall driving its train off its rails
To crushing Rousseau's Social Contract
Which colored many a dream
Wherein the Stars and Stripes
Flapped and took with them
The wind of change to the confines
Of the world and drew with their magnet
The best of what the world
Has to offer now trampled upon
By a bunch from Conrad's
Narcissus' forecastle
Wherefrom the ilk and his

Allow their imagination to run wild
And fertile to take
By hook or by crook
Human cargoes
Who against all odds
Have proven their worth
Developing wings to fly
And have had one of theirs perch
upon the house they built
Not as humans but a fraction
And a horde of wingless birds
And only good for domestication
Now pushing their abductors of yesteryears
To engage in fascination
With clinging on to the steering wheel
All to haste the second coming
Our creator requires no human consent
To haste though the former
Of Tsunami make their mission
To disperse the seeds of doubts
And taut their license to kill
And give free rein to cutting life short from innocence
All in the name of law and order
Out of which book he reads nothing
And understands absolutely nothing
Though he is a genius
And his results must be kept secret
Forgetting not he is the richest
Whose financial records
Cannot the light of day see
For all he proffers is nothing
But a French
Promise

With sole responsibility to him/her
Who in it believes
And not a poison pill
By the giver taken nor a bullet
With which he wishes to shoot
Himself on the foot
But would rather leave the field
Sprawling with indignation
That calls for pity
Even from far away
Myanmar and Cambodia
Taking in the sight of a giant
Once the apple of every eye
Now melting like ice
Under the desert heat
Coming from the hot air
Blown by a clown who has never
Of Descartes'
Cogito ergo cum
Nor of Pascal's
Defense of scientific methods
Heard
All of which the hulk ignores
And is propelled
to embracing charlatans
Musing only that which he thinks
And wishes not that which facts
Underscore and shine their light upon
To guide precision
Not his burning fire
Attracting none but those
Moths who distinguish
Not between fire and light

Wherewith the one destroys
The other gives life
After which all are endowed
With a will to choose
What to make
Or unmake
Mastering life
Or having life master
And enslave them
With the bitterness of a father
Whose gut is all bile
For the son dared to grow into a man
From the child of yesterday
When the latter the yoke bore
At the guise of the former
Now seeing the tables turned
And desiring a head-on collision
With the machines of democracy
Which laid the rails for the smooth passage
Of train's wagon after wagon
But when caught like a python
With the head in the booby-trap
Or a drunk driver with no license
Who would whip its tail and rant at factfinders
And stroke their enterprise
With the ugly brush
Of fake news syndicate
Hell-bent on a hit job
Directed against the one and only
Savior who can fix all
In such a way that at the end
There is none here to recall
Where it all started

With a climb down the stairs
Pitting us against them
Raced to the shores
By a hurricane of lies
Fully loaded in the brains of his base
Who in the brakeless train
Are unable to stop
And save life
But would go down with him
Into the abyss
Ramping through the political
Metal jacket
To place the windshield breaker
On the docket
With a sledge hammer in hand
To smash and let in
Katrina
Harvey
Sandy
Dorian
Andrew
Hugo
Wilma
Irma
Ike
Maria
Ivan
Michael
Florence
Rita
Charley
Matthew
Irene

George
Laura
Frances
And all in a gust
Akin to that which swept
The Romanovs' backyard
And painted the country
With their blood for many
Years and inherited by the ghoul
Now playing the puppet
Master
Pulling the strings of palatial intrigue
With trolls
Bought over by fear mongering
Chickens all squawking
In hope they bring down the eagle
As the train goes down
With them into the abyss
They enjoin the deceiver's
Offshoot and Faustus'
Master to craft to kill
Purity on the cross enflamed
By torch burning hooded hoodlums
Who find themselves empowered
By a driver with no compass
And with no binoculars
But with a hoarse roar that out-rumbles
The wandering locomotive
Choking and holding the earth's atmosphere
And stratosphere
And mesosphere
With thick mucousy smoke
Behind which he would hide

And pivot any question
Drawing his attention to call out
The horror he has bred and continues
To breed while undermining
The foundation on which stands the jewel
Of the West and perches on
Six Grandfathers' Mountain
Whereon leaders their marks have left
And a liar would he stole the show
Running his train against the site
With a barrage of blatant falsity claiming
That should Old Uncle Jo know
He would go and spoil the whole show
The lead liar would in his Jumping Train
Splatter with his bowel content
As he to his lying end comes
And is cornered by wisdom
Courage
Empathy
Sacrifice
Understanding
Generosity
Moral rectitude
Gravitas
Experience
Faith
Love
Honesty
Correctness
Foresight
Discernment
Care
Concern

Fortitude
Friendliness
Fatherliness
Obeisance
Resilience
All of which make the bricks
With which to build a wall of inclusion
Against the hate of the irate
Farther afield to the right
On board the new Hitlerian
Train and immoral conscience
Of America
Desirous to bring down
The beams of the gates
Of freedom targeting not
White
But
Mexicans
Blacksicans
Blacks
Browns
Yellow
Muslims
Chinese
Indians
And much more of whom both driver
And passengers hold are waste
From human blow off valves and smoke box and chimney
Come to steal from the grange
Where they have garnered grains
Exclusive to the taste
Of the non-pigmented
Who are skilled and astute

At defending theirs
Unlike the tinted
Who for a plate of rice
Would sell their messenger
Of goodwill and have him pilloried
To the joy of Pusillanimous Bulldogs
Called to stand back and by
And play wing breakers
Scaring away the olive branch carrying doves
'Coz a revelation has injected shockwaves
Down the mad driver's spine
Throwing him and his train in a feat
And off the rails and out of control
To head to the unlit city in the valley
Far from Wordsworth's Reaper's Vale
Filled with melodious echoes of a resounding
Golden voice from a solitary maiden
Whose would never send back
An invective of any form
That'd plunge a mourner
Into the depths of agony
That left Simone de Beauvoir
With eyes wide-open
To spot the classes into which humanity
In her own society
Is divided with mention
To clothes
Faces
Bodies
Smiles
Gaits
Interests
And occupation

With failure to talk
Of the diversity
Her society dichotomized
Based on the color of the skin
To ignite the persistent onslaught
Of deep rooted injustice
Brought to bear upon blackness
Whose moans
Groans
Growls
Grunts
Wails
Whines
Cries
And screams
Instead but bring home
Vilification and disgruntlement
Alongside threats of law and order
From a lawless tax
Evading profligate
Espousing to right a wrong
Is to double down on the same
That has blemished humanoids
From whence Cain chased out the breath
From his baby brother
For finding favor and fame
Where the former found disgrace and shame
For having allowed his anger and hate
To trump fraternity that ought to beget
One love that earns another
And warrants life in unity
Devoid of devious trickery
And irresponsible prideful denial

That bring swords to clink onto one another
And raise the flag of a deadly sin
Jimmy Cliff would call
Foolish pride
Jilting the grandfather of chemistry
Only to fall down and be picked up
By his grandchild who would scurry
The fallen in a copter
For respite that he wants to take away
From the taxpayer and being one
Who knows and feels not
The pinch of taxpaying
And does enjoy free loading
He accuses others of doing
And having come from their s… hole
Countries to steal the freedom
Cake baked for the largest mouths
That would vomit ceaseless volcanic lava lies
That even if made molten magma
Would fertilize no soil
In the footsteps of tradition of the greedy
Who never would suffer to rid a house rodent
With poison and of a sudden
They have become animal lovers
And especially those who love
The flesh in their plates
And would wash it down
With human sweat
Tears and blood
Not minding how many a black woman
Empties her tear gland content
Over the loss of her offspring
Snatched by licensed to kill

Masturbating renegades dressed in blue
To bring nothing but the blues
Which when thrown to their faces
As the result of white privilege
One of their pro-life bigots jumps from behind the pulpit
And would quickly insinuate
The existence of no such thing
But white blessings
And black curses
To be the root of the divide
Which clearly human is
Craftily shifted to a divine
Design
Which is rather a baby dove
And not belligerence by a branch
Ignited as a means to take others
Four generations behind with knees on the neck
For any time they a move make
To shift their stead
The leech would be with no host
And leave a noose around the neck
Of their choicest game of playing with the health
Of passengers who see not themselves
As such but allies and equal partners
In the enterprise of train wrecking
Happy trigger joy riders
Who unleash untamed reptilian
Predators preying upon bird eggs
And careful not to crush theirs
Notwithstanding their massive weight
Bearing upon bird eggs in quest for the truth
That will cut the highway
To the blood sucking reptilians

And remind them their weight
Unfit to destroy their own eggs
Which hatch they must hatch
For sowing seeds of wind
They must the monster storm harvest
And seeing the storm so near
They must some heat take off
Even by means of catching a virus
To invoke sympathy from birds
In readiness to fly
And kiss the heavens their executioner
Would everything do to have innocence six feet
Under in the pitch dark of hellish smoke
Preventing sight from embracing the sky
Where he belongs and not under the weight
Of their class hard at work
Trampling upon liberty
And justice for all as these two dare
Evoke Quakers and Levelers' Resistance
And pledge for egalitarianism
In any nation where God has been hijacked
And His name used to cage babies
Still kicking to get the smell
And taste of mammary juice
While their parents are sent packing
With tongues wagging with sweetness
The children are in the blissful haven
Of never-dreamt-of material things
To which they'd ne'er have been privy
In their parents' world of indigence
Where God is engraved on the hearts
And not on the currency
And their belief reduces money

To the bitterroot from which evil flows
To infect the stream of human consciousness
And make money makers
Mongering disciples
Wanting in the milk of human kindness
Which if available and impartially
Sliced for distribution
Would kill strife and groom
No gain the driver
Of the wrangling jumping train
To whom equity is stealing
From the rich to feed the poor
Which must be fought with tax breaks
To keep the poor where they ought to be
And fly the death-cult leader
On a topmast for him to thump his chest
For having beaten a dreaded virus
To which four hundred thousand plus and counting
Have succumbed and under his watch
Doing nothing but wishing
To such an end
All and sundry
Foe fiend or friend
Opponent or proponent
Unwilling or willing
With backs against his wagons
Or on board his train of doom
Collided and spared him the shame
Of having had to be sick
With a psyche that all along
Has been fooled sickness is weakness
And maddened by a dream
He'd let his contagion

Take the path of his jumping train
Off its rails for he cares not
'Coz as his grip slips
He must clench onto
His master's sly crawling incarnate
With whom he would this world
Reckoned the brakeless train
Transports to the incubating
Rose Garden
Blossoming with gatherers harvesting
Juicy fruits from the tree of denial
The mad and kleptocratic driver takes for one of knowledge
Just to exhibit his satanic bent
Slamming on the gas pedal
He takes for brake's
In hope to find those of the spirit
He'd long derided with a tight fist
Banging the table
And tooting
The very beginning
Of his own end
And no doubt welds
His own doom with his hands
Mouth
Nose
Legs
Fingers
Eyes
With his ears blocked
To joy
Peace
Love
Kindness

Goodness
Forbearance
Obedience
Faithfulness
Gentleness
Uprightness
And self-control
As the rails on which to take a joy ride
To eternity and not the injectable bleach
And senseless defiance of science
With the arrogance of a spoiled gnat
With neither wit nor might
Who clings onto the idea of power
As a birthright only money
Can confiscate and shut the rest
Or bully them to submission
In the manner of his puppet
String pulling put in master
Who had once run to his rescue
And unable this time with the wind blowing out
Of the closet every dirty little secret
Moving them
Step by step
Inch by inch
Toward the history books
Of tomorrow outlining
The first moron
To be given the helm of a train
And the first to have been so given
Without a policy or project
And one who has delighted
To play the driver for four years
During which scandal after scandal

Got him closer to the oubliette
Or cold house
He has always dreamt and held
Is the province of the scum
And sun tan hide
Not his ilk of cash caged patients
Living in a card castle in the air
Against which the driver his train runs
To peddle a groundless fiction
Stressing the health of the nation
He has always had come first
Which could not be farther
Afield from the truth
All in hope for the panacea
To halt the jumping train
In which everything is flipped on its head
And the driver and his conductor
Would we contended
With their impediments on the road
To vote as a toll free bridge
With nothing in common with the mastermind
Of Bridge Gate
Now in a fight against swimming
Across the river
Having been thrown out of the jumping train
And that for the second time
After serving once as a transistor
And viceroy heading a transition team
That brought to the quay
The dreadful train
With no sound of a guitar
But the cacophonous
Wrangling and jangling

Simply meant to confuse
By-standers and have discord
Reign
Amongst all who refuse
To suck up and jump on board
The trumpencean train of ineptitude
Flaunted for one able to propel to high altitude
And relegate boot licking scientists
To the background of the bottommost
Where a sick and mentally unhinged driver
Becomes mechanic and fits sparks plugs
To ignite the engine of hatred
He refuses to recognize
But calling that patriotism
Which hands out arms and munitions
To crime mongers
And pray they stand their grounds
In the name of that amendment
Which is far from being mine
Which holds the first place
But the eternal second which *ceteris paribus*
Should be a gift to law espousing
Citizens and not hooligans
Gunning for kidnaps and summary
Execution of all willing to serve
And serving as speed bumps and road blocks
To his brakeless train
On a helter-skelter swoop
Downhill
To throw a hand clapping prolife
Garbage bag on the scale
That has struck a balance for this nation
Warranting checks and balances

And now being coopted to steal the very right
Upon which the unsung founding father
In singing his own Paine
And raising his twain
Doubts contends
All others are dependent
To give the eagle wings to soar
And command and show the might
And true spirit curbing erosion
And preventing devastation
By the DJT derangement syndrome
That has gripped passengers on board
With some of his choir boys eager to jump off
The train as the choir maestro tells
The world he has not visited the driver's
Cabin in months and since finding out
The train driver had lost it
And taken the train off the rails
Honking for a rescue crew
To subvert justice and lynch
Surreal political foes whose lifelong
Enterprise has been service
Unbeknownst and unknown to the insane
Taking his flesh and bone
For iron and steel
He lied he'd bring back to business
When indeed he'd rebuff Coltrane's
Jazzy sax piping of Love Supreme
And dispossess any of a profession
Were he/she unwilling to have his/her bones
Shaken by the jumping train
And disinclined to sing the false cure
Proclaimed by madness

Having failed in business
And politics
And would now venture into the science of medicine
And cannot tell his SARS
Is Severe Acute Respiratory Syndrome
And were a high school pupil to ask him
What RNA was
He'd be quick to take a swipe at the youngster
For not knowing the NRA
Upon which he is dependent
Nor can he establish
That which constitutes antibodies
Replicase
And polymerase
Which underlie the SARS-CoVs
That he has made his sole train
In which delusional wagons lackeys sit and rock
To dirges they take for panegyrics
Lauding and applauding themselves for the catastrophe
It would have been had they not been fantastic
In handling
Hiding
And managing
The kakistocrat's cyclone of lies
That has torn apart an erstwhile
Beautiful beauty and dressed her in a monstrous gown
In trump's weaning days playing indolent boys
Shredding butterflies apiece
That the mad driver replicates axing the union
With machination into bits and pieces
And plunging the jumping train
Into a boundless identity crisis
Leaving Old Uncle Jo to pick up the pieces…

Printed in the United States
by Baker & Taylor Publisher Services